PUERTOS DE LUZ / HARBORS OF LIGHT

Puertos de Luz
Harbors of Light

Marjorie Agosín

Translated from the Spanish by
E. M. O'Connor

Introduction by
Anne Freire Ashbaugh

WHITE PINE PRESS / BUFFALO, NEW YORK

White Pine Press
P.O. Box 236
Buffalo, New York 14201
www.whitepine.org

Publication of this book was made possible, in part, by public funds from the New York State Council on the Arts, a State Agency; with funds from the National Endowment for the Arts, which believes that a great nation deserves great art; and with the support of the Amazon Literary Partnership, the Huntington Fund of the Wellesley College Spanish Department, and Wellesley College.

ISBN 978-1-935210-87-0

Library of Congress Control Number: 2015959246

Author's Acknowledgments

Books of poetry are often guided by the inexplicable, by illuminations that conjure images, sounds, tastes, and fragrances in the early stages of a work that then begins to be transformed and born.

I want to thank Judy Dworin, founder and artistic director of the Judy Dworin Performance Project, for encouraging me to consider the main dancer of her company as a beacon, a lighthouse. These poems are a tribute to her and to her illuminating choreography.

I'm grateful to Anne Freire Ashbaugh, who continues to inspire me with her wisdom and has always been able to put into words what I envision.

Thank you to E. M. O'Connor for her translation, Gabriella Wynne for the preparation of this manuscript, and for the constant encouragement of my friend and colleague Carlos Vega.

To John Wiggins—
my harbor

Table of Contents

PALABRAS DE AGUA / WORDS OF WATER

Introduction:
Unraveling Darkness

Anne Freire Ashbaugh

What is the meaning of life? That was all—a simple question; . . . The great revelation had never come. . . . Instead there were little daily miracles, illuminations, matches struck unexpectedly in the dark; . . . In the midst of chaos there was shape; this eternal passing and flowing (she looked at the clouds going and the leaves shaking) was struck into stability. . . .

Virginia Woolf, *To the Lighthouse*

This new collection of poems by Marjorie Agosín uniquely offers a poetic insight into an iconic symbol in literature: the lighthouse. In singularly beautiful poems, she unfolds new places for seeing, windows as wide as the sea, darkness that surrenders itself to the light of day, storms that shake the trees and those that shake the heart. All these elements offer themselves to the eye. In the tradition of great narratives that previously thematized lighthouses, in particular those by Edgar Alan Poe and Virginia Woolf, Marjorie Agosín repositions lighthouses to restore their prominence and expose their continuing literary power. The latter becomes apparent in the way Agosín integrates lighthouses into every aspect of life, including acts of remembering, loving, fearing, and nurturing. Thus, the collection importantly brings to the foreground the guiding lights contained in light towers and the guiding light of consciousness. Matter and spirit relate, as do shore and sea.

Usually, a lighthouse represents safety and order in the midst of immense dangers, like the threat of shipwreck during a storm. It awakens the hope of returning home unharmed at the end of a journey, and it promises stability in the midst of flux, what Woolf identifies as "this eternal passing and flowing" (*To the Lighthouse*, 135). In Virginia Woolf's narrative, the lighthouse itself constitutes a destination, a place for seeing and remembering. Like Virginia Woolf, Marjorie Agosín lets the lighthouse be a destination, yet for Agosín, the lighthouse is also what facilitates the journey and an inner light. As such, the lighthouse is both final and efficient cause in our lives so that without it, our lives would reveal only disorganization.

The window that in Woolf's novel guards solitude while threatening exposure becomes for Agosín a creative space as she writes that Penelope "sketched the world from a window." The window, furthermore, offers a possibility for relating to another in the darkness ("At night you pause, leaning out, you are a window"). Windows serve also as links between old houses and the universe because they "greet celestial visitors." Finally, it is on a window facing the woods that the fantastic love for a mermaid unfolds. While they relate deeply to the traditional symbols, these modulations accomplish much more. They capture the creative force of seeing.

Like Poe's four-day journal, written in a lighthouse—the fourth day left empty perhaps as an intimation of the narrator's death—Agosín, too, enters into a lightkeeper's perspective. Agosín's lightkeeper, however, writes in a "logbook of water" and the rain penetrates his very soul, washes the earth, and cleanses the self. In Poe's story, the lighthouse rested on a base made of chalk ("The Lighthouse," entry of January 3). In Agosín's poems, the light-house rests solidly on the earth or rock and within ourselves, shining with a dual light that promotes the union of spirit and matter symbolized by light-houses from the outset. Poe intimates the dissolution of the foundation. Agosín awakens a furious storm that disables electronic gadgets but restores intersubjectivity: "When the cellphone went mute, // the computer empty and dark, // I took your hand, // and you abandoned the machine. // You told me you would return to play with love."

Invariably, Agosín's poetry is transformative. What takes place in this collection of poems, however, is something new. She unravels the darkness. Her verses move light to the foreground even in landscapes populated by shadows. Light penetrates stormy shores, sleepless nights, pain, fear, deaths, fog, embodiment, and love. The light in this collection is not the light of understanding or revelation, though both understanding and revelation per-vade the text. The light in these poems is a guiding light. Thus, the collection itself serves as a lighthouse.

Ulysses' longing for Penelope spills through the whole book, steering toward safe shores all yearning for any and all loved ones, mother's stories, an old house, children peacefully sleeping, and countless memories. The night becomes long but propitiously so, and especially for those who love, write, or in some measure create life. Like the lighthouse of her mother's tales, the poems of Agosín invite us to adventure and risk but do not ship-wreck us. Individually quite beautiful, collectively, the poems are indomitable. When she writes that "El relámpago desnudó las raíces de los sueños pero no pudo con el amanecer," Agosín reveals her poetic power to wield light, however ominous, into a new element. Dawn conquers lightning and veers its light, now subdued, to guide away from harm. Less dramatic than the lightning, the dawn, the first appearance of light in the morning, is constant, fulfills the promise of daily life, and anchors readers in reality. Lightning pierces the darkness but it does not unravel it.

How do the poems in this collection, like the dawn, unravel darkness? In the poem "At night you pause, leaning out, you are a window," we observe a paradigmatic example of that unraveling. In the first verses, darkness vanquishes sight. Lost among all else that the darkness covers, we too are forced to surrender our lineaments, all individuality swallowed: "At night, you pause, ... you are a window // The window is like a world." Then, the rain falls "slow upon your fleeting hands," restoring through the sense of touch the individuality and the specificity of objects. The hands, ready to experience rain as petals, experience the softness and gentleness of night rain. In the form of petals, the rain begins to unravel the darkness by rendering its blindness harmless to the touch. Then, the menacing slowness of night, too, ceases to be frightening and becomes our teacher. Conceived simply as a matter of hours passing, hours that move toward dawn, the darkness of night becomes an opportunity to experience our own historicity in the passing of time. Not a dark scary place, but flowing time meets us at night. Night in fact, has its own light proper to its flight "through our hands" or of its passing. The passing of time that night reveals is in my hands: "You hold time within your hands. // Nothing slips out of them. // Nothing grows dark." What appears dark in the night is not really dark. Darkness is a passing aspect, not a feature of things. We retain light within our hands and use the darkness to free our imaginations. Toward the end, even the darkness of death emanates a guiding clarity that sheds light. The lighthouse, once more visible, is part of a garden and "Sign of plentitude // negation of emptiness." Providing greater safety still, the lighthouse becomes internalized. The first poem reveals how Ulysses' longing reaches to the lighthouses of Ithaca, but "It was their light that burned in his soul // like the lamps of the earth like the lights of all that is loved." Thus, loving, perhaps the riskiest of all human experiences, acquires in the poem a power to sustain an inner light that will guide lovers through any dangers. Within, the light relentlessly shines unquenched on any shore because it is ours. Just like Socrates' guiding voice, Agosín's introduction of an inner lighthouse or guiding light, arises within the soul of those who take risks and welcome the experiences and challenges that life itself offers. The troubled seas that Ulysses must face symbolize the challenges in question. Appropriately, we receive the light from a voice that matches the rhythm and constancy of the tides, a voice "that smells of sun" reveals to us that it is possible to return "to the lighthouse of your childhood.

// Your hands will hold its robes of sun." The first moment of inwardness, then, recaptures our values and our culture, experienced in our childhood, as guiding principles.

The poem that reveals our inner light, serves also as an inner light of the collection in as much as it is meta-poetical. Its title, "I approach the dream that is another dream within a dream," signals that feature. The poet has reached out to her inmost dreams, found the thick oneiric layers, and allowed the voice to affirm and to accept the inner light of memories. The poem closes announcing a "Lighthouse of origins // where the world names itself with colors" or with the most vivid recollections of sun shining fleetingly on our faces, "like a caress." From this perspective, each of the poems may be reread and relived and each reader may find a space where their inner light shines. Thus the collection not only gathers many poems, it invites multiple readings and generously speaks to all who read it. There is in this aspect of the book a literary magic proper to Agosín and very difficult to cultivate. It involves a process of writing poems that deeply express our own individual experiences while simultaneously connecting with the experiences of others. This intersubjectivity at the core of the work points also to another way of unraveling darkness. This is a path of philia or a distilling of the light hidden in the density of another person's love for us and our love for them. Consider the various layers of philia in the text. First we meet the heart-rending longing of Ulysses' love for Penelope and her enduring reciprocal love. A furious ocean separates them and the poems acknowledge the fearful storminess of the sea between them. Gradually, however, the monstrously vast ocean becomes a window, an innocent place from which to express their love: "The love of Penelope who waited, // who sketched the world from a window // the size of the sea." Simultaneously, the verses enlarge Penelope's window and shrink the distance

The second path of philia is maternal and introduced in the context of night stories through which the mother expresses her love for the children and through which she tames their fears by weaving for them the image of lighthouses: "Mamá tangled many lighthouse stories together // one into the other, until she wove a rough cloth // to blanket us from fear."

The bed of children's stories becomes the lovers' bed. Now the philia fears not the pain of longing but the promise of presence. Thus, in "At night on that far away island," a place supported by memories, bodies entwine and then surrender to a "sleep that was simple and close." Together, the lovers welcome the morning and observe the lighthouse, symbol once more of safely adventuring. Night, however, returns but the poem transforms the strong winds of stormy weather into "the light of the night flying through our hands." Present in memory the other awakens feelings and fears of the dark night when there will be only emptiness. The lovers, however, do not shipwreck. The lighthouse caretaker's "omen and presence" unravels the darkness of absence by his persistence. Likewise, the poem "In the dense night we open to love's desire" uncovers the erotic reciprocity of the lovers and unravels the darkness of the night. The poem fully entwines the lovers and the lighthouse in a dense but perfectly constructed image of lovers and lighthouse "bathed in a torrent of light."

In "Fog flying low and high," the lovers grow old together and experience the philia of reciprocal friendship. The fog plays with them and allows them to be both present and absent to each other. This contact pierces them to the core: "I call you and your hand sings, sings like an echo that sings. // The echo of my words are tangled in your hands. // We lose and find each other." The poem does not allow the fog to hide one from the other, even though they have "seen each other grow and age." In the closing verses, the "horizon clears" to allow the playfulness of fog to supersede fear of losing or being lost.

In, "Immobile, shrouded in fog," it is the space of love that lies hidden. The house had become the witness of enduring contact and aging together. Even after others inhabited the space, the house remains theirs because they "lived and loved so much inside it." It was the darkness of the house that allowed them safe light to discover each other and where their love allowed them to face even the darkness of death without fear. The lovers are any lovers, but they are also a young girl and a lighthouse keeper. This unravels in the poem "Among the oceans." The poem recalls the stories told by the mother to the children both in its narrative verses and in the familiar use of "Once there was a girl who fell in love // with the lighthouse keeper." As such, this poem gathers the two forms of philia in a fantasy of first love at a distance and all its promises. With it, ends the first part of the collection.

The second part, "Words of Water," unravels darkness through the power of words or logos. In this section, we can see the inner light at work. The opening verses of the section clearly delineate the unraveling in question: our inner light is the light of logos or language. We begin envisioning a conjunction of opposites: "Words of water // words like river stones." The opposites blend precisely because of the power of language to sustain reason even when confronted with an apparent contradiction. A metaphor (words of water) and a simile (words like the stones) do the hard work. Thus, we can see through these images that words flow but they support or sustain discourse, as do stones for someone crossing over the waters.

In this context, we are reminded of the lighthouse we carry within ourselves. The poem invites us to sleepwalk through the darkness and "perch upon the immense night" and to ask: what happens to words? Where have they gone, those sounds that once meant so much? Then, an extraordinary unraveling of darkness takes place. The darkness of silence, the emptiness of sound that veils the contours of words, is seen as a crucial ally of speech, one without which no sense could happen because there would be no room for pauses. Silence is shown to have a light, albeit semantic. When we speak we have to transform the darkness of pauses into a rhythm of signification. Logos, like Agosín's poems, orients itself towards light.

The path of logos and that of philia blend as the collection closes. In the poem "When words unravel," for example, we see this powerful conjunction and also an effective example of how the poems unravel darkness. The first stanza shows us logos itself unraveling, weaving and unweaving meaning: "When words unravel // when they say and unsay, // dissolving like the bodies, //that love one another." The bodies in love supplant the power of the voice to express themselves sensually, without words. No darkness can pierce their union, and thus, darkness dissolves. In their contiguity, bodies in love function as lighthouses unto each other while "there in long spells of silence." For the lovers, likewise, the darkness of night sheds its ordinary meaning to become a space of creating meanings. In the end, when the storm wind leaves them naked, when they are alone, they speak to each other only to promise they will "return to play with love." That assurance in the collection's last verse is its final promise of unraveling the darkness.

Ulises añoraba regresos
Ulysses Longed for Returns

Ulises añoraba regresos

Ulises añoraba regresos.
Ningún hechizo detendría el anhelo inagotable
de regresar a casa.

Ahí lo esperaba el augurio de las cosas conocidas.
Las granadas, como la fuente de las maravillas.
El ritmo del sol al atardecer, que lo bañaba de pertenencias
sobre la mesa dorada.

El amor de Penélope, la que aguardaba,
la que dibujaba el mundo desde un ventanal
del tamaño del mar.

Aunque el gemir del deseo lo cautivaba,
en los tiempos del desespero,
y el rugir desgarrador de los vientos,
perjudicaba el regreso,
era, como todos nosotros.
Añoraba a Itaca,
el hablar con sus muertos,
en la casa que fue la del padre,
visitar el cuarto de Telémaco mientras dormia,
y sentir el paso de Penélope
como un rumor de hojas y estrellas.

Lejana estaba Itaca la deseada y la cotidiana.
Lejanos los faros de una casa imaginaria.

Pero era aquella luz, que se encendía dentro de su alma.
como las lámparas de la tierra, como las luces de todo lo amado.
Eso era lo que marcaba el arduo camino a casa,
el regreso profundo,
donde todos y nadie lo conocían,
donde anhelaban con júbilo, con ira su regreso.

Ulysses longed for returns

Ulysses longed for returns.
No spell could confine his relentless
yearning for home.

The omen of familiar things awaited him there.
The pomegranates, like the fountain of wonder.
The rhythm of the sun at dusk bathing his belongings
upon the golden table.

The love of Penelope who waited,
who sketched the world from a window
the size of the sea.

And although desire's moan captivated him
in times of desperation
and the heartbroken roar of the winds
put his return at risk,
he was like all of us.
He longed for Ithaca,
to speak with his dead
in his father's house,
to visit Telemaco's room while he slept
and to hear Penelope's footsteps
like a murmur of leaves and stars.

Far away was his desired and everyday Ithaca.
Far away were the lighthouses of the home he imagined.

It was their light that burned in his soul
like the lamps of the earth, like the lights of all that is loved.
That was what mapped his arduous passage home,
the profound return
to where all and nobody knew him,
to where they anticipated his return with jubilation and rage.

Ulises soñaba con Itaca, la cauta y la bella,
con las manos de Penélope trenzando memorias.

Ulysses dreamed of Ithaca, captive and beautiful,
where Penelope's hands braided memories.

Por las noches mi madre me cuenta historias

Por las noches mi madre me cuenta historias.
La historia del faro allí en las costas
donde el ángel de los sueños guarda su umbral de agua.

Mamá enredaba tantas historias de muchos faros,
una sobre la otra, hasta que hiló una tela aspera
para protegernos de la dureza del miedo.

At night my mother told the children stories

At night my mother told the children stories.
The story of the lighthouse there on the coasts
where the angel of dreams guards her watery gate.

Mamá tangled many lighthouse stories together,
one into the other, until she wove a rough cloth
to blanket us from fear.

Por las noches te detienes, te asomas, eres una ventana

Por las noches, te detienes, te asomas, eres una ventana.
La ventana como un mundo.

El mundo como una ventana.

Miras la lluvia tenue, lentamente descender sobre la fugacidad de tus
manos.

Los pétalos de las que ya fueron rosas, descienden.
sobre el petalo de la noche.
Y es la lentitud, tu maestra.

El tiempo lo sujetas entre tus manos.
Nada se escurre.
Nada se oscurece.

At night you pause, leaning out, you are a window

At night you pause, leaning out, you are a window.
The window is like a world.

The world like a window.

You see the tenuous rain fall slow upon your fleeting hands.

The petals of what were roses descend
upon this hour of night.
And slowness is your teacher.

You hold time within your hands.
Nothing slips out of them.
Nothing grows dark.

La noche del relámpago

La noche del relámpago:
el estruendo, el sonido,
las campanas de la isla,
enmudeciendo de temor.
El relámpago derribó los sonidos.
El vacío del cielo,
dejó de ser.

La tormenta sobre la isla,
precipitada y salvaje,
quebró el sentir del tiempo,
derribó palabras,
invadió almas con un estruendo salvaje.

El relámpago derribó el tiempo de la noche,
y los fantasmas del cielo custodiados por las estrellas.
Tampoco pudieron deslizarse por la ruta estelar.
El relámpago desnudó las raízes
de los sueños
pero no pudo con el amanecer.

De pronto el sol, con sus quimeras,
acarició a los temerosos,
les devolvió lentamente la espesura de la luz.
El cielo y su familia de pájaros antiguos
transformó el sollozo en voz.
Llegó la claridad del día y la noche,
los invisibles volvieron a salir,
de sus temerosos escondites.
Visitaron al faro y al jardín,
regresaron a conversar con las bahías,
volvieron a soñar con el canto de los pájaros.

The night of lightning

The night of lightning:
the boom, the sound,
the bells of the island
made mute by fear.
The lighting struck down all sounds
and the vastness of the sky
was no more.

The storm over the island,
rushed and wild,
broke all sense of time,
knocked over words,
invaded souls with a savage thunder.

Lightning destroyed the weather of the night,
and the ghosts in the sky guarded by the stars
could not slip away through their stellar routes.
The lightning stripped the roots
of their dreams
but it could not touch the dawn.

Suddenly the sun, with its chimeras,
caressed the fearful, slowly
returned the thickness of light.
The sky and her family of ancient birds
transformed the sobbing into voices.
The clarity of day and night arrived,
and the invisible ones emerged
from their hiding places.
They visited the lighthouse and the garden,
they returned to converse with the bays,
and to dream once again about the bird songs.

Señal de la plenitud,
negación del vacío.

Sign of plenitude,
negation of emptiness.

De pronto se precipitaron las lluvias

De pronto se precipitaron las lluvias.
El sonido de sus aguas perpetuas
del cielo, descendían con fuerza,
sobre las pequeñas casas de las islas.

Alguien dijo que era imposible
protegerse de ellas.
Alguien dijó que no había ni tiempo
ni espacio para huir en la dirección de la luz.

Y así las lluvias siguieron cubriéndonos
con un sonido que se asemejaba al sonido del abandono.
También los pájaros gritaban mientras se alejaban de sus moradas.
De pronto llegó el gran silencio,
un silencio plasmado de vacíos...

Tan solo la oscuridad que entraba y salía
por las puertas selladas de las casas.
Hasta los pájaros caían en las orillas del mar,
sin cuerpo y sin historia.

La oscuridad del tiempo de las tormentas seguía rodeándonos
y se deslizaba apresurada
sobre las cosas llenas de luz
para reinar sobre ellas
en el tiempo de las cosas oscuras.

Pero alguien en una casa vecina, la casa cerca de la bahía
dijó que jugáramos
al arte de la paciencia,
que aprendiéramos a acariciarnos
en la oscuridad,
hasta que la iracunda tormenta
se fuese a otras islas.

Suddenly the rains rushed

Suddenly the rains rushed.
The sound of perpetual waters
descending strong from the sky
on our small island homes.

Someone said it was impossible
to protect oneself from the rains.
Someone said there was no time
nor place to flee toward the light.

And so the rains continued to cover us
with a sound that echoed abandonment.
The birds screamed and left their dwellings.
Then the great silence arrived,
a silence etched in emptiness...

Only darkness came and went
past every door locked tight.
Even the birds fell bodiless,
without stories to the shores.

And the storm's darkness surrounded us,
slid serpentine over anything full of light,
squeezing out the smallest spark
to reign over the island
in the time of dark things.

But in the house on the harbor,
a neighbor said we should play
at the art of patience,
that we would learn to caress
one another in the darkness,
until the storm took its rage
and left for other islands.

Por las noches en aquella isla

Por las noches en aquella isla,
isla de las memorias.

El viento llegaba desde lejos.
Llegaba a cantar la noche.
La noche le cantaba al sol.

La noche también le cantaba al viento.

Nuestros cuerpos reposaban sobre las costas imaginarias.

Eramos el cielo y la tierra,
la tierra y el cielo.

Nuestras bocas, estuarios.

La luna tambien llegaba a acompañar la noche
y entrabamos al sueño, sencillos y cercanos.

De pronto al amanecer decias,
"La tierra quieta está,
la luz del faro como rosa de oro."
Nos miraba quieta.

El obsequio de otro dia.

El cuidador del faro en la distancia,
augurio y prescencia.

Hasta que regresó la noche,
el tiempo de los vientos,
la luz de la noche volando en nuestras manos.

At night on that far away island

At night on that far away island,
island of memories.

The wind arrived from far away.
It arrived to sing to the night.
The night sang to the sun.

The night also sang to the wind.

Our bodies reposed upon imaginary coasts.

We were sky and earth,
earth and sky.

Our mouths, estuaries.

The moon also arrived to accompany the night,
and we entered a sleep that was simple and close.

At dawn you said,
"The land is still,
the glow from the lighthouse a golden rose."
In stillness we watched one another.

The gift of another day.

The lighthouse caretaker in the distance,
omen and presence.

Until night's return,
the time of the winds,
the light of the night flying in our hands.

Me acerco al sueño que es otro sueño dentro del sueño

Me acerco al sueño que es otro sueño dentro del sueño.

Junto a las mareas
una voz que huele a sol dice:
"Volverás al faro de la infancia.
Tus manos sujetarán sus cordeles soleados."

Llegará la luz de todos los orígenes
donde el mundo se nombra con colores,
señales del cielo descienden hacia el rostro.
La luz como una caricia que se escapa.

I approach the dream that is another dream within a dream

I approach the dream that is another dream within a dream.

Beside the sparkling tides
a voice that smells of sun says:
"You will return to the lighthouse of your childhood.
Your hands will hold its robes of sun."

Lighthouse of origins
where the world names itself with colors,
signs from the sky fall upon faces.
The light is fleeting, like a caress.

La niebla volando bajo y alto

La niebla volando bajo y alto,
contemplando los caminos del cielo y de la tierra.
La niebla que nos esconde y revela.

La niebla camina sobre nuestros cuerpos.

Te llamo y tu mano canta, canta como un eco que canta.
El eco de mis palabras, se enreda en tus manos.

Nos perdemos, nos encontramos.
Nos hemos visto crecer y envejecer.

El horizonte se despeja,
la niebla labra otros caminos.

La luz del faro, la luz de Dios.

Fog flying low and high

Fog flying low and high,
contemplates pathways through sky and earth.
The fog hides and reveals us.

The fog walks upon our bodies.

I call you and your hand sings, sings like an echo that sings.
The echo of my words is tangled in your hands.

We lose and find each other.
We have seen each other grow and age.

The horizon clears,
the fog trails other paths.

The light of the lighthouse, the light of God.

Inmóvil, arropada entre las nieblas

Inmóvil, arropada entre las nieblas,
la casa nos aguardaba.

Llegamos a ella, espesos de brumas,
como si ella fuese una embarcación en espera de pasajeros.

Sin temor, trepamos por las raídas escaleras,
sin temor, la mirada se acostumbró a una clara oscuridad.

Estaba ella, la casa clara, aguardándonos abandonada y dulce.
Entramos cautelosos.

Oímos pisadas y murmullos.
Alguien ya habitaba en ella.
Nos invitó a pasar.

De pronto, rafagas nublaron las paredes
y supimos que, como los enamorados, no podríamos vivir sin ella.
La adornamos de signos, de senderos invisibles.
Poblamos sus entornos con sirenas y duendes.
Hicimos un parque de luciérnagas para protegerla durante la noche.

Vivimos tanto en ella, nos amamos tanto en ella,
que nos costaba dejarla sola por las tardes.
cuando los búhos querían poseerla.

Pasaron los días sin calendarios.
Los árboles eran como un mar de hojas.

Nosotros nos descrubimos en ella,
envejecimos en ella.
Y sin temor a la muerte,
aun aguardamos los días y las noches.

Immobile, shrouded in fog

Immobile, shrouded in fog,
the house had been expecting us.

We arrived at her door thick with haze,
as if she were a ship awaiting passengers.

Without fear we climbed the worn steps,
without fear our eyes grew accustomed to a bright darkness.

The bright house was there to guard us, abandoned and sweet.
We entered with care.

We heard footsteps and murmurs.
Someone already lived in her
and invited us in.

Suddenly gusts clouded the walls,
and we knew as lovers do, that we could not live without her.
We adorned her with signs to invisible paths,
invited mermaids and elves to live alongside her.
We made a ring of fireflies to protect her through the night.

We lived and loved so much inside her
that it was hard to leave her in the evenings,
when owls wanted to swoop inside.

Days without calendars passed inside her.
Outside the trees were like a sea of leaves.

We discovered each other within her,
grew old in her rooms.
And unafraid of death,
we still bide our days and our nights.

Ella nos ampara.
Es también anciana y vulnerable.
Sus puertas son un misterio.
Por sus ventanas llegan visitantes celestiales.
Es nocturna y danza.
Es diurna y sueña.

Como nosotros, que no anotamos ni horas ni días,
que se nos olvida hasta nuestros nombres,
que a veces nos llamamos por otros.
Pero no el de ella la casa clara, la casa como un cielo.
Casa entre el agua y el bosque,
entre el cielo fecundo y la tierra aérea.
Casa querida puerto cercano,
ilusión de puerto.

She shelters us.
She too is weak and vulnerable.
Her doors are a mystery.
Her windows greet celestial visitors.
She is nocturnal and dances.
She is diurnal and dreams.

Like us, unaware of hours or days
until we forget our own names,
and sometimes call each other by others'.
But never forgetting the house clear like a sky.
House between water and woods,
between the fecund sky and the aerial earth.
Beloved house nearby port,
illusion of a harbor.

Íbamos cruzando las espesuras del camino

Íbamos cruzando las espesuras del camino.
La niebla se hundía entre nuestros pies,
y trepaba veloz por las hendiduras de los ojos.
El ruido incesante de los días en las ciudades manejadas
por la velocidad de diminutos aparatos controlando
el paso del tiempo, de la vida.

Atrás habían quedado.
Huimos de ellas, esas maquinas veloces,
que determinaban el paso del tiempo.
Queríamos otra soledad,
retornar al ritmo del faro.

Íbamos dejando atrás el peso de los días de ocio
para entrar a un bosque espeso,
para entender el majestuoso y sutil ruido de los signos.
Donde de pronto algo se aparecía,
donde lo desconocido ya era familiar,
donde los ruidos eran de follajes y pájaros,
donde navegábamos alados y livianos.

Atrás aquellas luces, las devoradoras,
las asesinas, las luces de los diminutos teléfonos.
Allá, todo lejos al más allá de la voracidad del espanto.
Allá han quedado ellas las maquinas devoradoras.
Y nosotros aquí en una isla que la llamaremos
la isla de la casa clara,
la mas antigua de las noches,
y tú me cuentas de aquella noche en la isla de Rodas.

Cuando de pronto alguien iluminó el mar con una canasta de fuegos.
Aquí tu me miras, aquí yo te miro y somos.
El ruido es tan sólo el parpadear de los ojos.

When we were crossing the thickets on the path

When we were crossing the thickets on the path,
the fog sank between our feet
and crept through the hollows of our eyes.
The incessant noise of the city besieged
by quick and tiny gadgets driving
the passing of time, the passing of a life.

We left them behind.
We fled those quick machines
that determined the passing of time.
We wanted another solitude,
to return to the rhythm of the lighhouse.

We were letting go of the weight of idle days
to enter into a thick forest,
to understand the majestic and subtle sounds of signs.
Where suddenly something appeared,
where the unknown was already familiar,
where the noises were foliage and birds,
and we navigated with light wings.

Behind us were those lights that devoured,
the assassins, the lights of the tiny telephones.
There far away was the voracity of fright.
There the devouring machines had remained.
And here on an island we named
the island of the clear house,
on the most ancient of nights,
you tell me of that night on
the island of Rhodes.

When suddenly a basket of fire illuminates the sea.
You look at me, I look at you, and we are.
The noise is only the blinking of our eyes.

Aquí te reconozco

Aquí te reconozco,
somos por fin nombres, aguas, mareas.
Hemos venido a buscar trozos de sombra y luz.

Somos navegantes sin GPS.
Somos bosque somos luz.

Here I recognize you

Here I recognize you.
We are at last names, waters, tides.
We have arrived to look for pieces of shadow and light.

We are navigators without GPS.
We are forest, we are light.

En la noche densa nos abrimos a los deseos del amor

En la noche densa nos abrimos a los deseos del amor,
hacia el agua que nos cubre cual frazada de estrellas.
Toda la noche, el tiempo transcurre sin premura,
hasta sentir el llamado del faro.

Entre las más oscurecidas mareas,
el faro nos llama y nos recibe,
en la soledad de las piedras y las marejadas.
El faro se abre para nosotros
cual cúpula sagrada
bañada en un torrente de luz.

In the dense night we open to the light's desire

In the dense night, we open to the light's desire,
to the water that surrounds us like a blanket of stars.
Throughout the night, time passes without haste,
until we feel the call of the lighthouse.

From among the darkest tides,
the lighthouse calls and receives us
in the solitude of the stones and the tides.
The lighthouse opens for us
like a sacred spire
bathed in a torrent of light.

Lentamente, furiosamente la niebla llega hacia las costas

Lentamente, furiosamente la niebla llega hacia las costas.

Vuela bajo como una historia aún no dicha,
una historia que aun no se hace.

De pronto como un encantamiento o una maldición,
la niebla nos circunda.
Las manos de la niebla elongadas
hasta llegar y cercar nuestras cinturas.
Nos cubre, nos desnuda y nos descubre.

¿Quiénes somos cubiertos en la niebla que murmura?

¿A donde irán nuestros pasos?

¿Y esa luz arriba hacia el norte?
¿También vestirá los ropajes de la niebla?
¿O también la niebla podrá devorar la luz?

Luz como una promesa.
La luz de Dios sobre las aguas.
La luz como un día sin noche.

Slowly, fiercely the fog arrives upon the coasts

Slowly, fiercely the fog arrives upon the coasts.

It flies low, like a story not yet spoken,
a history not yet made.

And suddenly like a spell or a curse,
the fog surrounds us.
The fog hands elongate
to reach around our waists.
It covers us, unclothes and discovers us.

Who are we, wrapped in this murmuring fog?

Where will our steps lead?

And that light above, pointing north?
Will it also wear garments of fog,
or will the fog also devour its light?

Light like a promise.
God's light over the waters.
Light like a day without night.

De pronto y como de sorpresa

De pronto y como de sorpresa,
sin aviso,
la lluvia salvaje con su vestido eléctrico
nos despertó de nuestro espeso sueño,
eradicó la raiz del primer sueño.
El devorador llegó,
borrando los mapas del cielo,
llenandolos con las melodías de violines descartados.

Nos arrastró el clamor del viento,
sus cadencias, sus aullidos.
Era la lluvia, limpiadora del mundo.

La que amenazaba a los barcos de la guerra.
La que alivianava el pasaje de pequeñas embarcaciones.

Lo inesperado nos enseñó,
que también lo salvaje tiene su dulzura.

Y así la majestuosa sonora lluvia,
silenció el sonido del beso,
governó los nuevos mapas del cielo.

Desde la lejania, el cuidador del faro,
escribió en su cuaderno de agua.
Contó así que la lluvia visitaba su alma.

Y aprendimos de tiempo en tiempo,
sobre el agua y sobre la fe,
de las estrellas sobre las aguas,
en el tiempo de lluvias luminosas,
en un tiempo cuando la lluvia nos limpia,
mientras la lluvia llora.

Suddenly and by surprise

Suddenly and by surprise,
without warning,
the savage rain in her electric dress
woke us from our thick sleep,
eradicated the root of the first dream.
That devourer arrived,
erasing maps from the sky,
filling them with the melodies of discarded violins.

We were swept along by the wind's clamor,
by its cadences and howls.
It was the rain that cleansed the world.

The one which threatened ships of war.
The one which lightened the passage of small vessels.

The unexpected taught us
that the savage could be sweet.

The majestic, sonorous rain upon our bodies
silenced the noise of kisses,
sovereign over the new maps of the sky.

From afar the lighthouse keeper
wrote in his logbook of water
that the rain visited his soul.

In time we learned from time
about water and about faith,
from the stars above the waters,
in a time of luminous rains,
in a time when the rains cleanse us,
as they cry.

Después de las iracundas tormentas

Después de las iracundas tormentas,
escuchas el cantar del agua,
la danza de las algas marinas,
la bocina del faro,
que te vió entrar y salir
del sueno y la vigília.

Después de aquellas tormentas,
el tiempo de la plenitud,
la danza de lo que es,
y no es.
Las manos que en un gesto
de apertura
reciben al mundo,
como a una flor.

After the raging storms

After the raging storms,
you hear the rain sing,
the seaweed dance,
the siren of the lighthouse
that saw you come and go
from vigils and sleep.

After those storms,
comes the time of plenty,
the dance of what is
and what is not.
With just one gesture,
your hands open,
receive the world,
like a flower.

Entre los océanos

Entre los océanos,
otros océanos.

Entre la espesura del agua nocturna,
otras noches.

El viento cabalgando, trayendo cantos,
tan llenos, tan vacíos.
Escuchamos aquellas voces lejanas,
voces traídas desde el viento.

Tú, niña pequeña y sabia,
te has enamorado del cuidador del faro,
el que vive en la más desalamada de las soledades.

Por las noches lo saludas con tu mano imaginaria.
Y pareciera que tus diminutas manos,
tocan el cielo que es el otro mar.
Y más allá del cielo,
si es que hay otros cielos,
el guía de la noche te cuenta cosas,
como la más vasta imaginación de su amor
que a ambos los bendice
que te trae mas cerca a los sueños del amor
en la vasta noche.

Tú, desde la más dulce de las distancias
le preguntas si conoce el nombre de las estrellas,
si conoce tu nombre.

Among the oceans

Among the oceans,
other oceans.

Among the water's deep nights,
other nights.

The wind gallops, swiftly bringing songs
so full, so empty.
We listen to those far away voices,
voices carried by the wind.

You, small and wise girl,
fall in love with the lighthouse keeper
who lives in such heartless solitude.

At night, you greet him with your imaginary hand.
And it seems that your tiny hands
touch a sky that is another sea.
And farther from the sky,
if there are other skies,
the guardian of the night tells you
the vast imagination of his love
that blesses you both,
draws you closer to dreams of love
in the vast night.

You, from the sweetest distance,
ask him if he knows the names of the stars—
and does he know your name?

Había una vez una niña que se enamoró
del cuidador de un faro.
O de una estrella.
Le escribió poemas de amor.
Que ardían como la luz de los días
en las costas imaginarias del amor.

Once there was a girl who fell in love
with the lighthouse keeper.
Or with a star.
And she wrote him love poems
that burned like the light of day
off love's imaginary coasts.

Palabras de agua
Words of Water

Palabras de agua

Palabras de agua,
palabras cual piedra de rios.

Te acercas sonámbula en la rapsodia de esta noche azul,
incierta de los lugares por donde viajas.

¿A donde regresas cuando la noche furiosa te saca de aquella quietud?

De pronto te inclinas en la noche tan inmensa.
Las estrellas fugazes como melodias en el cielo cercano,
y te recuerdas del faro dentro de ti.
Ese faro que invita a descansar en su luz,
el faro entre los océanos.

Ya sabes a donde van las palabras.

Naciste para contar historias.
Sabes a donde van las silabas.

Ese faro te añora.

Como una casa que espera tu llegada,
una casa habitada y plena.

El faro en la distancia te llama.
Te presta una mano.

Es tan cercana a la tuya y al cielo.

Y así viajan las palabras hacia la luz.

Words of water

Words of water,
words like river stones.

Sleepwalking the rhapsody of a blue night,
uncertain of the place you are nearing.

To where do you return when furious night expels you from that quietude?

Suddenly you perch upon the immense night,
fleeting stars like melodies in the neighboring sky,
and you remember the lighthouse inside you.
The lighthouse that invites you to rest in its light,
the lighthouse among the oceans.

You already know where words go.

You were born to tell stories.
You already know where the syllables go.

That lighthouse longs for you.

Like a house awaiting your arrival,
a house inhabited and full.

The lighthouse in the distance calls you.
It reaches out its hand.

So close to your hand and to the sky.

And your words travel toward the light.

Hemos elegido vivir aquí en esta isla innombrable

Hemos elegido vivir aquí
en esta isla innombrable,
en esta isla cuyo nombre se asemeja
al silbido de los pájaros que la circundan.
Aquí en la isla de los pájaros,
hemos aprendido a vivir,
junto al ritmo de las aguas,
a tejer la luz del amanecer,
con todas las penumbras de la noche misma.

Aquí en esta isla,
hemos calmado los deseos
de acumular, de envidiar, de herir
a los que más amamos.
Aquí no hay odios de otros tiempos,
la memoria se desplaza entre la luz.

We have chosen to live here on this unnameable island

We have chosen to live here,
on this unnameable island,
on this island whose name resembles
the whistling of nearby birds.
Here on the island of birds,
we have learned to live
with the rhythm of the waters,
to weave the light of dawn
with all the shadows of night.

Here on this island,
we have calmed our desires
to acquire, to envy, to wound
those we love the most.
Here there is no hatred from other times;
its memory is scattered in the light.

Aquí en la isla

Aquí en la isla
somos como los pájaros,
que sobre ella vuelan para custodiarla.
Los pájaros a nuestro alrededor son nuestro paisaje.
Atrás habíamos dejado el tiempo de la ira
para regresar al tiempo de la paz,
a conversar con el tiempo del mar y de sus aguas,
a reposar con las salidas y las entradas de todas las aguas
a vivir más y más en el ahora,
en el tiempo del amanecer y la penumbra.

Here on the island

Here on the island
we are like the birds
that fly above to guard her.
The birds around us are our landscape.
We have left the time of rage behind us
to return to the time of peace,
to speak with the rhythms of the sea and her waters,
to rest with the comings and goings of the waters,
to live more and more in the moment,
in the time of dawn and shadow.

Toda aquella espesa noche

Toda aquella espesa noche,
toda aquella noche sumida en los oscuros sueños.
De pronto en la isla,
llegaron los pájaros.
Toda la noche,
oíamos el cantar
de aquellos pájaros en el silencio de la noche misma.

Y eran ellos, los soberanos,
del agua y del silencio.
Yo te dije que quería
siempre vivir en esta isla.
Rodeada de la dulzura del canto de estos pájaros.

Yo te dije que empezáramos
a amar el silencio,
para algún día aprender a cantar.
Como los pájaros que llegaron
a la isla,
como los pájaros que nos obsequiaron
el saber.

Y algún día, te dije,
que aprenderemos a perdonarnos
para volver a amar.

Throughout that thick night

Throughout that thick night
submerged in dark dreams,
the birds suddenly
arrived on the island.
Throughout the night,
we heard those birds' songs
in the silence of the night.

And they reigned, sovereign,
over silence and waters.
I told you I wanted
to live on this island always,
surrounded by the birds' sweet song.

I told you we should begin
to love the silence,
and someday learn to sing.
Like the birds that arrived
on this island,
like the birds who gifted us
with their knowledge.

And someday, I told you,
we will learn to forgive ourselves
and love again.

Nosotros, los que vinimos aquí en busca de amor y luz

Nosotros, los que vinimos aquí en busca de amor y luz,
nos encontramos claros y lucidos como un anillo.
Nadie supo porque llegaron a la isla.
Nadie supo si huían de la soledad de aquellas ciudades de humo.
Nadie supo reconocerlos,
mientras parecían aves sonámbulas,
siempre en dirección hacia las orillas del mar.

Tal vez traían en ellos el vigor de la envidia
y venían en busca de una hebra de luz
para aligerar aquel dolor que en sus almas llevaban.

Atrás habíamos dejado aquellas ciudades
donde nadie sabía amarse,
donde las palabras llevaban los atuendos del vacío.
Huimos a las islas en busca de la luz del alma,
para yo también nombrarte y decirte
amor del alma mía.

Y en las islas junto a los pájaros que habitaban en ellas,
que custodiaban nuestro sueño y nuestra vigilia,
aprendimos a tejer el tiempo del silencio.
Aprendimos a preservar las cuencas de la luz,
que después de las tempestades siempre salen.

We who came here in search of love and light

We who came here in search of love and light
found ourselves clear and shining like a ring.
Nobody knew why they came to the island,
if they had fled the cities of smoke.
Nobody could recognize them,
while they seemed like sleepwalking birds,
always moving toward the shore.

Maybe they held a vigorous envy within,
and came in search of a strand of light
to lighten the pain they had packed in our souls.

We had left those cities
where nobody knew how to love,
where words wore vacant vestments.
We fled to the islands in search of the light of the soul,
so that I could name you and call you
love of my soul.

And inhabiting the islands with the birds,
that watched over our dreams and vigils,
we learned to weave the moments of silence.
We learned to protect the wells of light
that the storms always leave in parting.

Toda la noche el cuerpo del amor

Toda la noche el cuerpo del amor,
con los dos cuerpos amados.
Sueñan el sueño de las aguas sedosas,
de la luz intermitente,
en la cercanía distante.
Toda la noche, el faro.
Y los cuerpos que se aman
en pleno deleite.

Se nombran los unos a los otros
con el arte de las palabras.
Que son océanos silenciosos.
Esa misma noche silencio.

All night the body in love

All night the body in love,
with two beloved bodies,
dreams the dream of silk waters,
of intermittent light,
in the near distance.
All night the lighthouse,
and the bodies that love,
delight in each other.

They name each other,
with the art of words,
that are silent oceans,
that same sea-night silence.

Cuando las palabras se destejen

Cuando las palabras se destejen,
cuando dicen y no dicen,
disolviéndose como los cuerpos
que se aman el uno al otro.
La luz del faro ahí, toda la noche.

Un cuerpo se encuentra con el otro.
En el sueño de la cercana y distante luz,
con misteriosa presencia,
los cuerpos que se aman, antiguos,
sabios en las cosas del amor.

Están ahí, en los encantamientos del silencio.
Con palabras que hablan entre los espacios
entre ellos florecen.
Con los secretos compartidos, lo que germina
las piernas entrelazadas cual hojas de otoño,
reconociéndose el uno al otro en las fronteras
del amor que se hace que se deshace.

When words unravel

When words unravel,
when they say and unsay,
dissolving like the bodies
that love one another all night,
the light of the lighthouse is there.

When a body meets the other body,
in the dream of near and distant light,
of mysterious presence,
the bodies that love are ancient,
wise in the ways of love.

There, in long spells of silence,
with words that speak in the spaces
between them, blooms
from the secrets they share, sprouting
from legs entwined like autumn leaves,
the recognition of the other in the borders
of love and love unraveling.

Amé la suavidad de sus palabras

Amé la suavidad de sus palabras,
como los intersticios del silencio.
Amé esa luz tan dentro de él como un
faro que me rescataba de los abismos.

Amé su luz que también se hizo mía.
Él era mi puerto, yo una bahía que él iluminaba.
A veces era una embarcación frágil
como los barcos de papel de los niños amados
y dibujábamos el principio,
y el fin de las estrellas.

El me decía que también la luz de sus ojos algún día se iría
y yo la recogería.
Como recojo todas las noches
las estrellas fugaces,
las que emiten su luz desde la claridad de la muerte.

I loved the softness of his words

I loved the softness of his words,
the spaces of silence between them.
I loved the light deep inside him,
like a lighthouse that pulled me from abysses.

I loved his light that also became mine.
He was my port and I was the bay he brightened.
Sometimes I was a fragile vessel
like paper boats beloved children made
as we sketched the beginning
and the end of the stars.

He said someday the light of his eyes would leave
and I would gather it,
like I do every night
the shooting stars,
those that shine from the brightness of death.

Como viajeros extraviados

Como viajeros extraviados,
bailamos entre el agua y tierra.

A veces pretendemos que el cielo,
era el mar y el mar, otro cielo.

Extraviados, danzamos entre ramajes de niebla.
Nuestros dedos señalando hacia el faro.

Brilló opalino sobre la espuma del agua marina.
Nuestras manos trenzadas la una hacia la otra.

¿Quién nos reconoció después del viaje?
¿Quién nos sujetó para encontrarnos?

Like wanderers adrift

Like wanderers adrift,
we danced between water and earth.

Sometimes we pretended that the sky
was the sea and the sea another sky.

Adrift, we danced between drifts of fog.
Our fingers pointing toward the lighthouse.

Shining opal in the sea-spray mist.
Our hands braided together.

Who recognized us after our journey?
Who pulled us in so we could find ourselves?

En tus ojos

En tus ojos
navego por la tierra.

En tu boca,
llego a todos los estuarios.

Tus manos cruzan las mías,
libres de objetos falsos.

De promesas naufragas,
tan sólo el rostro como un mundo.

Un oasis nos protege de las falsas pertenencias
y el manantial del amor cae sobre nuestros ojos.
El cielo llora celestes lagrimas.

Hemos llegado a las islas,
las que tienen serpentinas y antorchas.
Y el viento nos canta.
Y el agua una gran frazada.

Es refugio y crisálida:
somos.

In your eyes

In your eyes.
I navigate the earth.

In your mouth.
I arrive at every estuary.

Your hands cross mine,
free of false objects.

Free of shipwrecked promises,
just your face like a world.

An oasis protects us from false possessions
and a fountain of love falls upon our eyes.
The sky cries celestial tears.

We have arrived at the islands
that have streamers and torches.
The wind sings to us.
The water swaddles us.

In its refuge and chrysalis:
we are.

Se enamoró de una sirena

Se enamoró de una sirena,
la que estaba en un escaparate,
en una ciudad nevada.
En una ciudad donde las aguas regresaban
con el regreso de las nieblas espesas que todo lo cubrían.
Hasta la luminosa profundidad de las aguas.

La sirena tenia una cola,
negra como la noche espesa.
una cola como un mundo en movimiento.
Sus ojos eran celestes,
como los faros que guían a la noche misma.

Se enamoró de la sirena.
de aquel escaparate,
donde pasó desapercibida por tantos años,
donde nadie la miraba ni siquiera de reojo.

La empaquetaron
de cartones tan oscuros como la niebla misma de la ciudad.
Se la llevo a casa.
La puso frente a la ventana,
frente a un bosque nevado
donde tal vez antes era un mar.

Y el hombre tan solo,
el hombre solo ocupado de inventar números,
se enamoró de ella.
La quisó cuidar.
Limpiaba su cola color noche
pero no encontró nombre para ella.

He fell in love with a mermaid

He fell in love with a mermaid,
the one in the snowy store window,
in a city where the waters returned
with the return of thick fogs that covered
even water's luminous depths.

The mermaid had a black tail
thick as night,
a tail like a world in motion.
Her eyes were sky blue,
like the lighthouses that guide the night.

He fell in love with the mermaid
in the store window,
where for so many years she stayed unseen,
where no one looked at her, not even a glance.

They packed her in a box
dark as the city fog.
He brought her home.
He put her in the window,
a window facing a snowy wood
which perhaps was once a sea.

And this solitary man,
who only liked to invent numbers,
fell in love with her.
He tried to care for her,
cleaning her tail, the color of night.
But he couldn't find a name for her.

La nombró *mi sirena*.
Por las noches acariciaba su cola de noche.
Al amanecer, secaba sus lagrimas celeste
de sus ojos celestes como un faro.
Un día sintió que la debía regresar
al agua, que su cola,
color noche necesitaba bañarse
entre las olas y las algas.

Y así el hombre solitario
aprendió que también el amor, era dejar ser,
dejar partir.

Aquella mañana gris, en las costas grises,
el al despedirse le beso sus parpados
que lloraban lagrimas celestes.
Y la dejo irse entre clara y oscura.
La sirena emprendió su viaje
a un lugar que el aun ni siquiera imaginaba.

Entendió el arte de dejar ir,
también el amor era un dulce abandono.

Y regreso a su casa solitaria
aferrado al recuerdo de aquella sirena—
 a quién vio en un escaparate de una ciudad perdida,
y que le enseñó el arte de amar que es el arte de dejar ir.

Allí en las cercanías del agua,
en las costas lejanas y cercanas,
donde un hombre solitario y humano amo a una sirena
y la dejo regresar al fondo del agua.
Allí donde un faro perdido la esperaba.

So he called her *my mermaid.*
In sleep, he caressed her scales.
At dawn, he dried the sky blue tears
from the lighthouse of her sky blue eyes.
One day he felt she should return
to the water, that her tail,
the color of night, should bathe
between the algae and the waves.

And thus the solitary man
learned love can mean letting things be,
letting one leave.

That grey morning on the grey coast,
to say goodbye he kissed her eyelids,
that cried sky blue tears.
He let her leave between light and dark.
The mermaid began her journey
to a place he couldn't imagine.

He understood the art of letting go,
and that love was sweet abandonment.

And the man returned to his solitary house
clinging to the memory of his mermaid—
the one he saw in a store window in a lost city,
who taught him the art of love and letting go.

There in the nearness of the water,
in the far away and nearby coasts,
a solitary and human man loved a mermaid
and let her depart to the depths of the water
where the lost lighthouse awaits her.

De pronto la tormenta furiosa nos dejó desnudos

De pronto la tormenta furiosa nos dejó desnudos.
El refugio no estaba en el pequeño celular amarrado a tu mano.

No habían señales que emitían de esas maquinas diminutas
que parecían estar cosidas a nuestros brazos.

No había señal.
No había GPS.

Estábamos tan solo nosotros,
vulnerables como si nos hubiera llegado el terremoto del alma.

Y el teléfono celular mudo.
Y la computadora vacía y oscura.

Te tomé tu mano,
abandonaste la maquinita.

Me dijiste que volverías a jugar con el amor.

The furious storm left us naked

The furious storm left us naked.
Refuge was not found in the cell phone stuck to your hand.

Tiny machines tied to our arms
sent no warning signs.

There was no signal.
No GPS.

We were alone when the earthquake
struck inside our souls.

When the cell phone went mute,
the computer empty and dark,

I took your hand,
and you abandoned the machine.

You told me you would return to play with love.